Sally's Hard Day

By Christine Losciale-Thoemmes
Illustrated by Dr. Marissa Robinson

Copyright © 2016

Gr8self, LLC
San Francisco, CA/Denver, CO

ISBN:
978-1-5356-0365-2

This book is dedicated to
Children around the world,
And the child in us all.
May you find sunshine
On a cloudy day.

"I am having a hard day today.
Nothing seems to be going my way"
Said Sally getting ready for school.

When she ran for the bus
The sky was all foggy…

On the way to her room,

Where she was sent to go...

Sally STOMPED up the stairs

And she stubbed her big toe.

She plopped on her bed
And she felt even sadder.
Soon her mama came up
And asked what was the matter?

Sally shared all her troubles,
All her sorrows and woes.
She told her of breakfast,
And of friends and big toes.

Mama hugged her and smiled
And said, "I think I can help.
This is what I do
When such troubles are felt…"

"When I'm feeling angry
Or just plain upset,
I do things that can help me
And can help you too I bet."

"First I find a quiet spot,
I may sit on the floor,
Then I take a deep breath,
And I do it once more."

"With my hand on my heart
And a smile on my face
I just breathe in and out
At a slow steady pace."

"As I breathe in and out,
I continue to smile.
I begin to feel better,
Still I sit for a while."

"I keep my eyes closed,
And I quiet my mind.
I sit in this pose,
And I take my sweet time,"

Sally just frowned and thought,
That can't be true,
Breathing won't help me,
What will that do?

Part of her wanted
To whine and to SCREAM...

If she acted that way,
She could cause a big scene!

As she sat beside Mama
Feeling lost and confused,

She knew deep down inside
The right answer to choose.

She tried screaming and tantrums,
And was not feeling better.

She knew running away
Could not be the right answer.

Sally looked at her mama
And she let out a sigh…
She thought, maybe it's time
To give something new a try…

So she listened to Mama,
And tried what she said.
She breathed in and out,
Clearing thoughts from her head.

With her hand on her heart
And a smile on her face,
She breathed in and out
At a slow steady pace.

She let her anger float away
Like the clouds in the sky,
Allowing peaceful thoughts in
To fill up her mind.

Sally's worries were lifting
She could think straight again.
Then she smiled at Mama,
"This was helpful" she said.

So the next time you wake up
And things don't go your way,
When you're feeling quite angry
Or you're sad or afraid…

Just remember this trick,
The one Sally learned to do,
You just breathe in and out
And it helps you pull through.

You will find when you're done
Things seem not quite as bad.
You may even forget
What was making you mad.

Note to Reader

- Smiling releases endorphins, which has a positive effect on mood.
- Slow steady breathing increases relaxation and decreases stress.
- Closing the eyes eliminates distractions and encourages relaxation.
- Hand on the heart is a centering gesture of self-love.

Christine lives in Castle Rock, Colorado with her husband and 4 children. She has Master's degrees in both Psychology and Creative Writing and is a certified Life Coach. She enjoys teaching Yoga and reading to children.

Marissa lives in San Francisco, California with her husband. She has a PhD in Psychology, specializing in Art Therapy. She is a licensed therapist and teaches Mindfulness.

www.ingramcontent.com/pod-product-compliance
Lightning Source LLC
Chambersburg PA
CBHW041602070526
44586CB00003BA/52